MY MOM
A PHOTOLOG BOOK

Created by Janet Horowitz and Kathy Faggella

Illustrated by Steve Jenkins

Stewart, Tabori & Chang
New York

Your mom is an important person in your life. You probably know her very well, but wouldn't it be fun to know more about her? Wouldn't it be interesting to know what her favorite things are, and in which ways you are alike? Wouldn't it be fun to be able to give your opinions and comments about Mom as you see her?

You can! Here is the opportunity for you to have fun as you get to know your mom even better. With this book, a camera, film, and a little time spent with Mom, you can learn a lot about her and about yourself as well. You can be a photographer, reporter and writer of your own PhotoLog book about you and your mom.

Uses for your **My Mom** book:

- Use **My Mom** as an ice breaker—it will open up discussions and conversations with Mom and the whole family.

- Use **My Mom** to think about comparisons between your life and your mom's, the ways you are alike and how you differ. Maybe you can find the reasons why this is so.

- Use **My Mom** to make connections with your mom. When you realize that you enjoy the same things, you can do them together.

- Use **My Mom** as a gift for your mom. She would be thrilled to have a book written all about her (and you)!

- Use **My Mom** as a treasured memory book, to help you remember all the special times you spent together with your mom.

Some hints to help you complete your book:

1. Take photos.
Be prepared to take photos of your mom that will fit the photo captions. One roll of 24-print film will be enough for this book. Try and take candid photos of your mom. You will also need two old photos of mom.

2. Talk with your mom.
In between the picture taking, interview your mom about the things that you notice. Ask questions when you think of them or write them down so that you won't forget to ask her later. Listen carefully to the things Mom tells you and others. Listen to the stories that friend and relatives tell you about your mom.

3. Fill in this book.
When your pictures are ready, decide which ones would best fit the photo captions and pages of this book. Then complete the pages. Some answers can be found by watching and observing, others from talking with your mom. Follow the order in this book, or skip around, whatever makes you feel comfortable. You do not have to fill in everything. And remember, have fun!

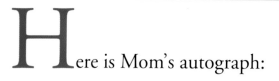

Here is Mom's autograph:

My mom's autograph is (check):

☐ small ☐ fancy ☐ easy to read
☐ large ☐ plain ☐ hard to read
☐ neat ☐ delicate
☐ messy ☐ firm

Mom's autograph is like her because:

_____

_____ .

Mom's
Family
Tree

Mom

Mom's broth[er]

Mom's sisters

Mom's mom

Mom's dad

Mom's uncles

Mom's aunts

Mom's granddad

Mom's grandmom

Mom's granddad

Mom's grandmom

Write the names of
Mom's relatives
on each branch.

Mom's uncles

Mom's aunts

Mom was born on _____ in the town of
_____, in the country of _____.
She went to school at a place called _____
where her nickname was _____. She says
she was a _____kind of student.
When she was growing up, she wanted to be _____
_____.
After school she _____ _____
_____ _____.

I was born on _____.

Mom says when I was a baby, my favorite thing to eat was

_____.

My favorite toy was _____.

My first word was _____.

Mom remembers me as this kind of baby (check):

☐ friendly   ☐ shy   ☐ funny
☐ demanding   ☐ active   ☐ happy
☐ curious   ☐ noisy   ☐ _____

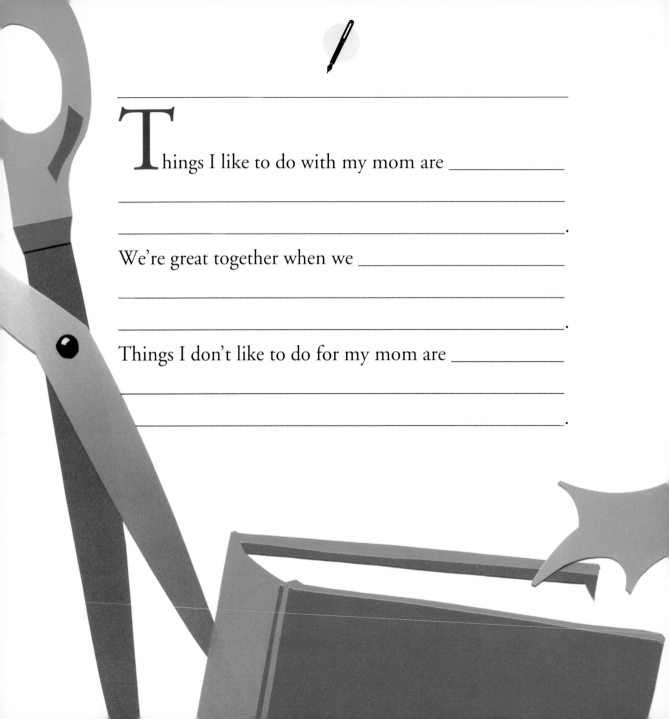

Things I like to do with my mom are _____
_____
_____.

We're great together when we _____
_____
_____.

Things I don't like to do for my mom are _____
_____
_____.

If Mom were an animal, she'd be a _____ .

If she were a toy, she'd be a _____ .

If she were a flower, Mom would be a _____ .

Mom gets out of bed at (fill in hands):

I get up at:

When I'm at school, Mom usually _____
_____.

Mom spends the evenings _____
and I _____.

Mom's bedtime is: My bedtime is:

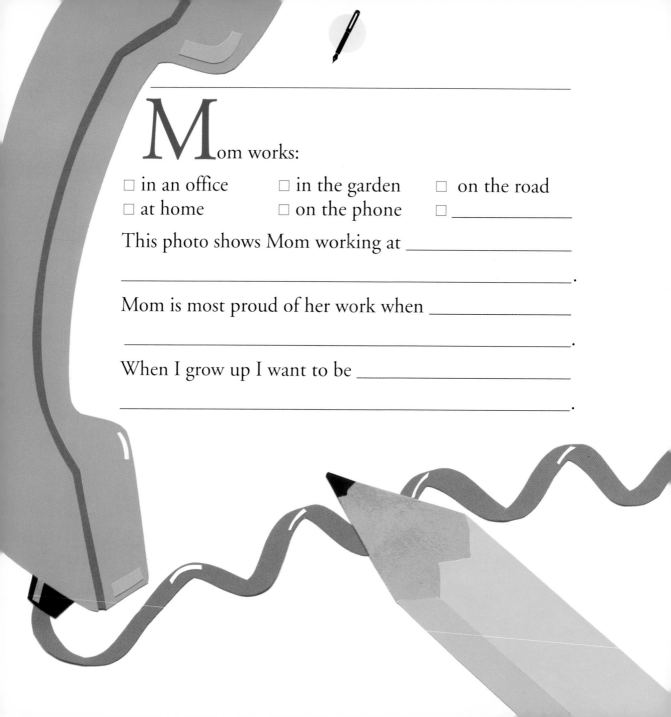

Mom works:

☐ in an office   ☐ in the garden   ☐ on the road
☐ at home   ☐ on the phone   ☐ _____

This photo shows Mom working at _____
_____.

Mom is most proud of her work when _____
_____.

When I grow up I want to be _____
_____.

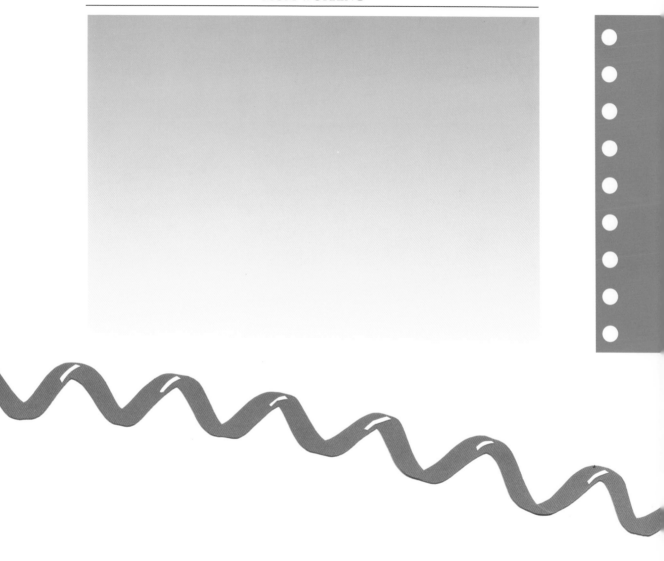

Shoes can tell you a lot about your mom. Mom wears these types of shoes for:

_____

_____

_____

_____

_____

Mom says her favorites are _____

because _____

_____ .

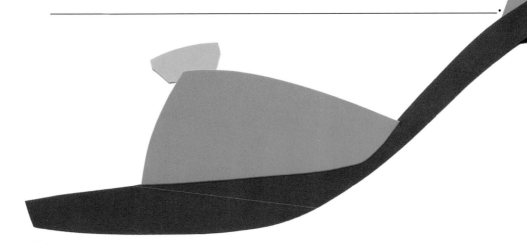

Mom spends her weekends:

- ☐ shopping
- ☐ cooking
- ☐ gardening
- ☐ sleeping
- ☐ traveling
- ☐ exercising

- ☐ visiting friends
- ☐ working
- ☐ watching TV
- ☐ sunning
- ☐ doing hobbies
- ☐ cleaning

- ☐ helping others
- ☐ worshiping
- ☐ doing errands
- ☐ painting
- ☐ repairing
- ☐ _____

Of all her weekend activities, the one Mom likes best is

_____ .

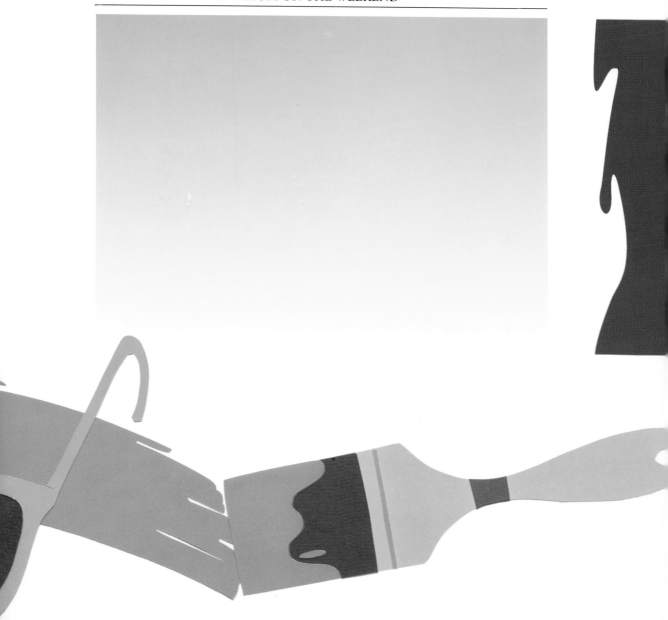

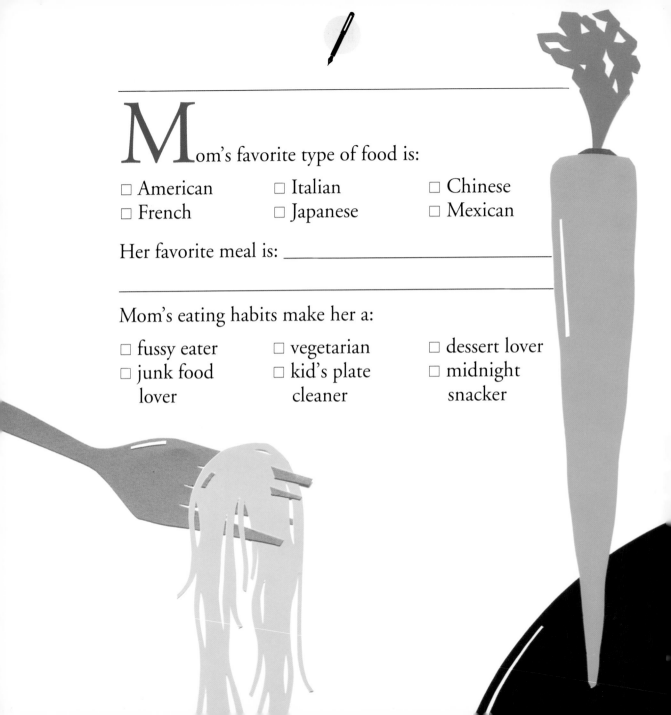

Mom's favorite type of food is:

☐ American ☐ Italian ☐ Chinese
☐ French ☐ Japanese ☐ Mexican

Her favorite meal is: _____

_____

Mom's eating habits make her a:

☐ fussy eater ☐ vegetarian ☐ dessert lover
☐ junk food ☐ kid's plate ☐ midnight
   lover   cleaner   snacker

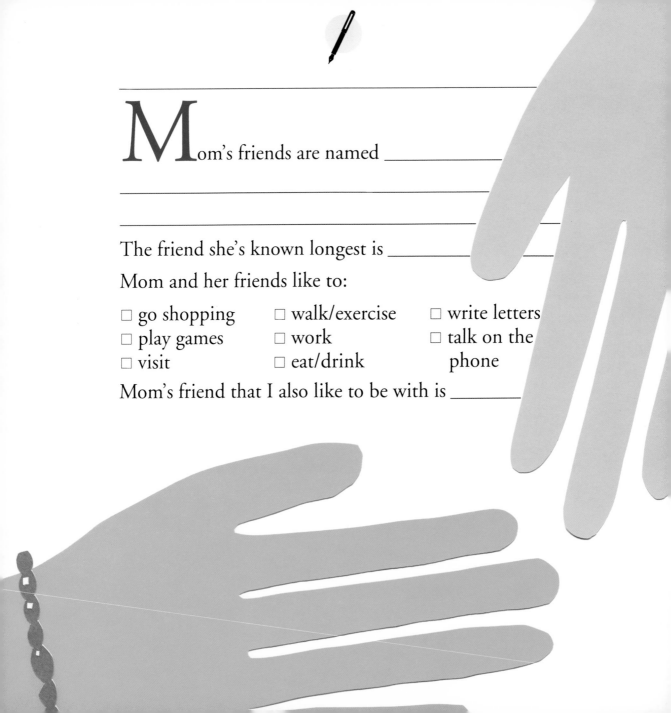

Mom's friends are named _____

_____

_____

The friend she's known longest is _____

Mom and her friends like to:

☐ go shopping ☐ walk/exercise ☐ write letters
☐ play games ☐ work ☐ talk on the
☐ visit ☐ eat/drink phone

Mom's friend that I also like to be with is _____

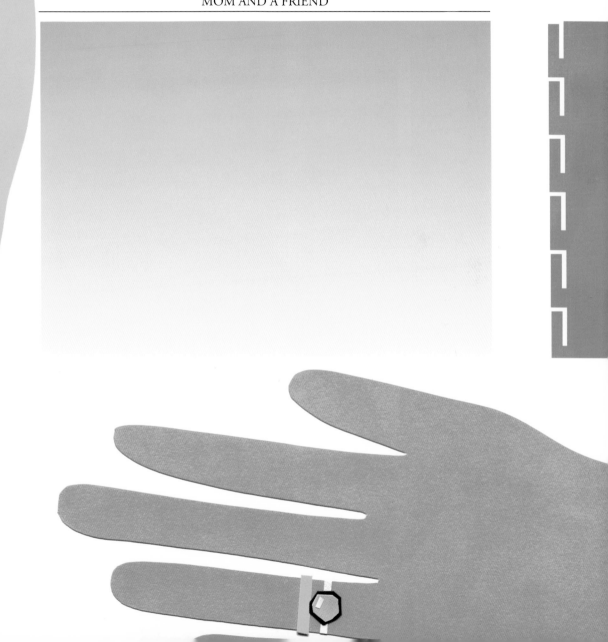

M om's favorite sport to play is _____.

Her favorite sport to watch is _____.

A game Mom and I like to play together is _____

_____.

Mom exercises when she _____

_____

_____

_____

Mom's favorite kind of jokes are _____

_____

Mom and I joke about _____

I always laugh when Mom _____

_____

This picture makes me laugh because _____

_____ .

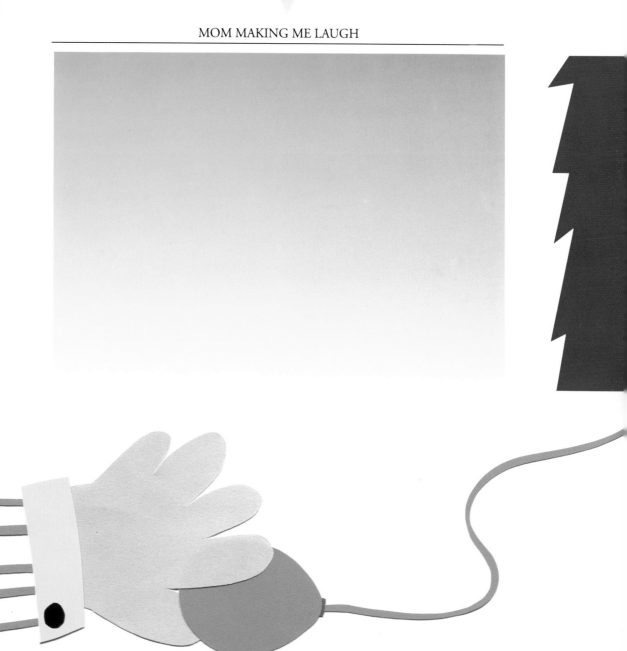

List and compare favorites:

Mom's		Mine
_____	Movie	_____
_____	Book	_____
_____	TV Show	_____
_____	Music	_____
_____	Color	_____
_____	Season	_____
_____	Holiday	_____

On a scale, our favorites are:

☐ (very different)   ☐ (similar)   ☐ (very much alike)

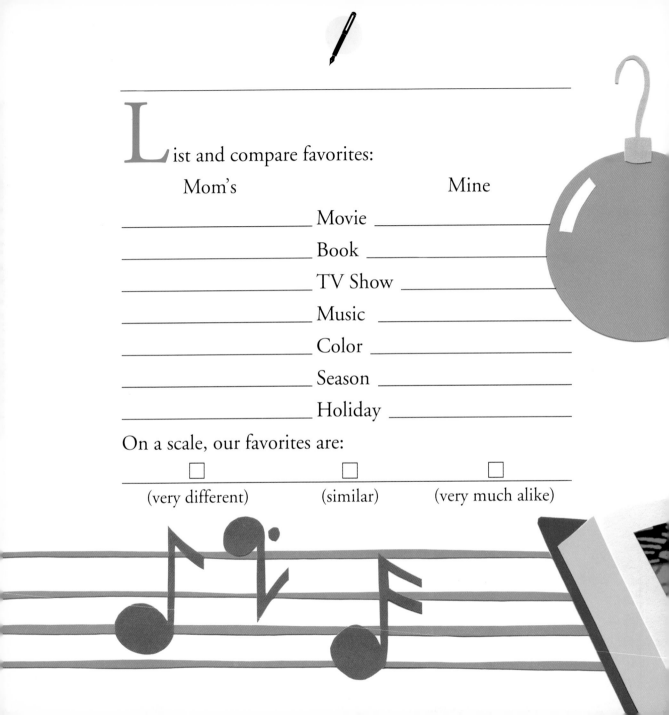

Check the ways that you see your Mom and yourself.

MOM	ME		MOM	ME		MOM	ME	
☐	☐	energetic	☐	☐	fun-loving	☐	☐	shy
☐	☐	talkative	☐	☐	smart	☐	☐	moody
☐	☐	caring	☐	☐	adventurous	☐	☐	serious
☐	☐	nervous	☐	☐	creative	☐	☐	musical

I think I'm most like my mom when_____

_____.

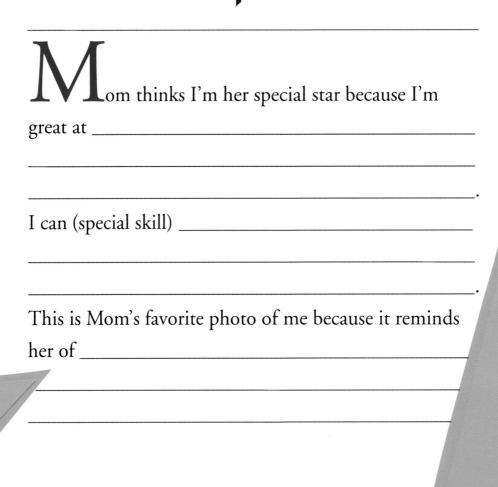

Mom thinks I'm her special star because I'm

great at _____

_____

_____.

I can (special skill) _____

_____

_____.

This is Mom's favorite photo of me because it reminds

her of _____

_____

_____

Happiness for Mom is _____
_____
_____.

Mom is happy when I _____
_____
_____.

Mom is happy in this photo because _____
_____
_____.

Some of Mom's goals are _____

_____

_____ .

Mom wishes she could _____

_____ .

Something that Mom never did but would love to try is

_____

_____ .

If she could change something, Mom would _____

_____

_____ .

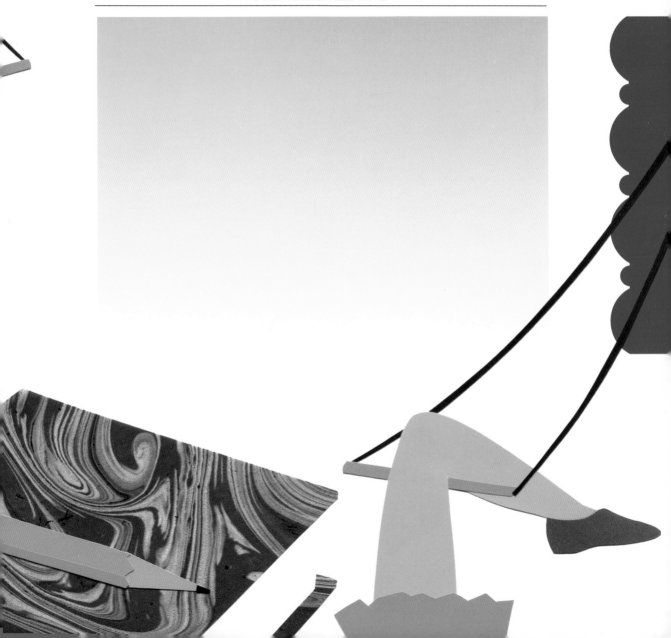

M_{om is:}

M _____

O _____

T _____

H _____

E _____

R _____

Mom's favorite saying is: _____

_____

_____ .

The M. O. M. (Most Outstanding Mother) Award goes to Mom for _____

_____.

Mom deserves recognition for her special skill of _____

_____

_____.

Mom gets an extra hug for _____

_____

and extra thanks for _____

_____.

AN AWARD I MADE FOR MOM

Design by Jenkins & Page, New York, NY.

Art Photography by Gamma One Conversions, New York, NY.

Composed in Adobe Garamond.

Type proofs by Graphic Arts Composition, Philadelphia, PA.

Printed and bound by Toppan Printing Company, Ltd., Singapore.